Honest Water

Also by Robert Farnsworth

Three or Four Hills and a Cloud

Honest Water

Robert Farnsworth

Wesleyan University Press
Middletown, Connecticut

Again for Georgia, and for Nate,
and to the memory of S.B.C., 1889–1988

The author wishes to thank the editors of the following periodicals, in which these poems, often in earlier versions, first appeared: *The American Poetry Review,* "The Carp That Swallowed a Diamond," "Toward Hallowe'en"; *The Antioch Review,* "Museum"; *Canto,* "Uses of the Cedar"; *Carolina Quarterly,* "Broadcast," "History," "Waterworks," "Your Left Hand"; *Crazyhorse,* "Against Snapshots"; *Ironwood,* "Night Game"; *Michigan Quarterly Review,* "The Pose"; *The Missouri Review,* "Blueprint," "Landscape for an Antique Clock," "A Postcard in Memory of Donald Evans," "William Cowper" (as "For William Cowper"); *New England Review and Bread Loaf Quarterly,* "At a Sunday Concert," "On Leaving a Demonstration to Have My Hair Cut"; *Ploughshares,* "Rooms by the Sea"; *Poetry Northwest,* "Almost Family"; and *Seneca Review,* "Destination," "Upon a Fit of Laughter."

I wish to thank George Colt, Alice Fulton, Fred Muratori, Ira Sadoff, and especially Arden Neisser, for their advice and encouragement.

All inquiries and permissions requests should be addressed to the Publisher, Wesleyan University Press, 110 Mt. Vernon Street, Middletown, Connecticut 06457

LIBRARY OF CONGRESS
CATALOGING-IN-PUBLICATION DATA

Farnsworth, Robert, 1954–
Honest water.

(Wesleyan poetry)
I. Title. II. Series.
PS3556.A725H6   1989   811'.54   88-28080
ISBN 0-8195-2168-X
ISBN 0-8195-1169-2 (pbk.)

Manufactured in the United States of America

FIRST EDITION

WESLEYAN POETRY

Contents

I

Broadcast

At dawn his voice was delectable,
forming vegetables from thick
Boston vowels and a gentle stutter.
Before the sun had cleared the scrub oak
he was off and running his cadences
over the air, an auction of pith
and fragrance, so many cents a bushel.
Dwelling an instant on artichokes, musk-
melons, leeks—he tumbled over the pears,
plums, peaches, lemons, oranges.
His voice comes back today
while I am filling postholes with loam
gone fine as cinnamon: once corn silk,
rinds, eggshells, grounds and cobs.
I'm still tuned in, and still can't think
without touching, holding words
to the thick, acquisitive, worldly
sides of the tongue. With his voice
I would gather those that urged
hockey games toward the final siren,
those that promised favorite songs,
or called to complain of landlords,
Lodges, laws, and terrible trades.
Hello, you're on the air. . . .
When I was bored I'd inch the dial
gravely down the frequencies,
composing a world of fragments.
Far in my secluded room, I heard
the nation breathe all night; under its
armor of lights and airline routes,
I heard it listening. And after hours
that radio would heat up under the pillow.
Now the old compost heap has cooled
and grown violets. In the lowest layers,

where leaves have lost their shapes,
worms incorporate their dank cities.
Barefoot in the wet grass, morning
sunlight firm on my shoulders, I stand
over this cart full of loam and listen.

Waterworks

Our moods do not believe in each other.
—Emerson

I

The bridge is a correction
of its image on the pond.
Only a string of shadow
slung around a stick suggests
this water moves,
until here at my feet it's
suddenly collapsing. . . .
Vapors float among the ferns.
The blood,
going and returning,
claimed and released,
can't bear this motion, sickens
watching water always swift
on solid stone.
It doesn't matter that down the ravine
the river recollects itself
and idles into forest.
Back on the pond's smooth face,
someone's shadow moves
like a sweep hand over the bridge.

II

Under the ripple of ice
on a gently sloping sidewalk,
water mingles with air
to spin downhill.
Bubbling black tears and gaudy fish
distend and wriggle,
ovoid, corpuscular,
joining up and sliding away
in pockets. Footsteps
have stressed complex stars in the ice.
All day that mobile

tapestry stays in mind,
diatomic, bacterial, a black-and-white
pantomime beneath a plate of ice
that says all day
get on with it.

III
Small pleasure lingering
on the bridge with Sunday's paper.
Bells let drift some song from the hill.
Green silt quivers
in nets of light below,
and shallow water toils through
a supermarket cart.
Six budding locust shoots
have forced out of the flood wall,
their leaves insisting on the current.
Between two thoughts I steady here,
and the comfort I took last night
from setting our table returns,
facing what was approaching sunlight,
lucent water and bells,
the melody now taking shape
through rich overtones.

Almost Family

Twilight slants up from the lake like rafters,
culminating somewhere above the broken clouds.
When I arrive, I follow it upstairs,
and lay my coat on the bed with the others.
The medley of prescriptions and perfumes
on the dresser brings back childhood evenings:
making myself a demon with mascara,
whispering over labels in the cabinet, safe
so long as mother's friend downstairs
kept shrieking over each new hand of cards.
The pile of coats is still strange—cool
satin sleeves and smoked collars—but none
is impossibly large for me now. After going
through the pockets of each without motive,
knowing even a trifle would have to be left,
I'd pile them all back in order—why, as
mother said, tempt fate? Voices surge again
beneath the floor. I am expected, will soon
be missed, and so run fingers through my hair,
open one more shirt button. Down there
some story, slang, or accent will place
each one of us—age and origins—as surely as
its carapace identifies the turtle. But up here
in the empty coats, the angels linger, unevolved,
invisible, everyone we thought to become,
almost family. My hand heats on the railing,
following another argument down the stairs.
I was once a thief in heaven, it begins.

Manifest

That coming back to the willow,
which still suggests itself to certain
words the wind will always comb
through it—that returning
to savor its flung, fountaining
midstream leaves, swung just
there beneath my eaves, beneath
those bricks precisely composed
as chimneys against blue sky—
that the view should give such
pleasure after five weeks'
absence might, beyond renewal,
say *home*, here's where I belong,
upstream in this dilapidated,
green New England town, whose
cool morning silences I treasure.
In the vertical light of the West
I walked, pale, observant, perhaps
a little dour, but still struck by
wonders I thought memory might
burnish and arrange. But like
the shells my China-trading ancestor
lugged home—cowries, whelks,
and murex, chambered, stippled,
polished in pastel—they're incoherent,
piecemeal sums of pale light
nobody can sort. What I saw, what
are now synaptic sparks, I would
praise to resurrect their frissons:
a jade lizard tasting air,
stitched white along the spine,

swallows suddenly arrowing up
into little urns they'd glued
beneath an overpass, tidal
galleries cut in tall escarpments,
some seabird's heraldic wings
shaken out on coppered water.
How shall I design this cargo list—
merely by returning with it
to a familiar life, to the willow
framed in view from my chair?
What shall I let it convince me
to believe? A man owns all that
he surveys, wrote Emerson, even
as he is owned by it. Patience,
says the willow, trust in gradual
revelation, fact as spirit's emblem.
Settle yourself, like that old
Congregational captain, among
products of pure looking—the mute,
unimprovable manifest of blessings.

Man Leaving a Florist

after Wyatt

They smile at him that otherwise would pass
Without so much as a lifted eye, smile
At him and those flowers under wraps.
What they know of his reasons they also
Know of spring: streets shining with brief
Rain, loose, rich odors, light beginning to last.
Rendezvous, the package says, sweet flattery—
They read it like a book in which their hopes
Are strangely echoed. But he hates
Buying flowers, always taken for a dope
Who won't spot a shriveled blossom 'til too late,
Until the water's fresh glissando in the vase.
And the clerk is always profoundly annoyed
When he insists upon *that* one. Here,
In this early evening street, he can't avoid
His good intentions, his thought that wants
To count—he can see it like a misbuttoned shirt
In the eyes of strangers. *How does her dear*
Heart best like it? He only remembers her
Heels' dint on the floor overhead, and the test
Pattern's rigid petals, looming in the dark.

Inferences
for Jack

By midnight I have put aside my book
to watch the ceiling: lacewings
unfolding, a crane fly curling its fragile
inch of abdomen into a cup hook. And moths,
as always beating their wings to dust
on a forty-watt bulb. Dances one can only
describe. But stop one pair of moth wings—
pin them open—the perfect specimen
will signify the whole frantic species'
devotion to light. Though there are mullions
more or less on every tenth camouflaged
wing, we've names for the moths, vernacular
and Latin; field guides know how common
or rare they are. Nature lives by repeating
herself. Our various words would translate
her profusions once and for all. On a porch
like this four summers ago, we had long talks
about talk, about obliquities and fragments
we all so easily make sense of: *Where's mother?*
someone asks, and hears: *There's a sale down
at Woolworth's.* What enables the questioner
to (ignore squabbling yellow budgies, bins
of plastic shoes, the postfan streamers,
the popcorn smell and) understand the reply?
So many environments we move in will not
plainly answer us—rich or threadbare
premises: non sequiturs tossed back
over shoulders, bleached wingbones
and one deserted nest, theatrical silence,
condensations of sorrow in a chord. . . .
No matter how many crane flies someone
has observed, imagination lets us believe
they all fast for the final summer stage
of their lives. Professing to know, we

admit how much we must imagine to know.
And evening conspires with us, comes
to keep its word, as if it knew that every
accurate word is a promise kept.
But it's a fragile arrangement—between
the mind and what molts and flutters from it.
Linnaeus lost his own name to a stroke.
Now we must infer each other from telephone
calls, occasional letters and visits.
This, then, must be something I neglected
to say—fond, grateful, meant to suggest
that creation sometimes speaks through us.
Some nerve or blood vessel flutters in my leg.
So much to follow. . . . The insects go on
pulsing overhead, as if across the screen
of some clairvoyant instrument. Commending
whatever I'll discover to you, I will get up
and walk until my eyes adjust to darkness,
believing summer's every perfect word.

Destination

At two each day the driver-
education car pulls up
to browse beneath our maple,
idling in shadows. Behind

the wheel a youth is bent
on behaving. Hand over hand
he grinds the gravel under
his tires, looking back

down the road's green vault
to a stop sign. He stares
a long time, as if something
might materialize from all

that empty pavement,
suffering his retrospective
so long the instructor begins
to doubt his sincerity

or reason. But as he dallies,
his turn signal holds the whole
town in place like a postponed
resolution. Think of us old,

lingering in a modern age we
don't understand, our wisdom
consisting only of such trivial
predictions—every one

promising those following
that we'll be turning in,
just up there, where the maple
used to burn in October.

Against Snapshots

I suppose it is a bad picture anyway—
too much contrast and awkward composition.
But a keepsake of the face that fills
the corner, whose arm along the lower frame
bends as if in benediction, to adjust the pair
of glasses atop her head. Hired to sit
this house a week, I have wakened daily
to this picture on the wall. Things are
as I see them at first light: in a white gown
a woman kneels, extending one gracious hand
toward something in the grass, something
unprovided by the eye. At the dark
lawn's edge shines a pond of lilies.
What pleasure day after day, discovering
her again in the foliage and clouds behind
that casual gesture—until the actual
face must be labored into focus, until I don't
bother anymore, until I'm keeping house for
nobody I know. Things are as I see them
in the undecided light. They will not photograph.

Second Elegy

Down among the rocks today
watching kelp inhale the swells,
the tide rip under a causeway,
I almost had it back to keep.
Among peninsulas of spruce
the salt hay had tarnished, and in sluggish
convolutions the estuaries distilled November light.
For a moment I had it back,
that contentment my shoulders
couldn't name but knew.
While it held me I didn't know whether
to call what I'd lost composure or despair.
I sat beside a pool,
watching through its rippled lens
an asymmetrical crab exploring a ledge.

People were feeding change
to the telescope installed on the cliff above,
swiveling its mask along the horizon.
But I had no use for the ideas of wave
confused at that flawless line—
I had the homesick shudder
intact, the room in your house, empty all winter
until I'd unpack and push the bed
right under the cold window.
Then I'd walk down into the breeze, to the beach
that was another room:
a clutter of gravel and mussel shells
that suggested only modest voyages.

Such clarity my petty sorrows gave that beach.
If I were still myself you'd still be there,
sowing birdseed across the snow.
A blurred column of heat would rise from the old ashcan.
Freezing shallows would clench my boots.
Now just inarticulate blood
can pronounce those joys.
Down at the Atlantic's edge today
I watched the sea, shunting, roiled in clefts of granite,
climb back up the tangle of rope
it had knotted under the rocks.
Today I almost had you back.
Then you were nothing, a distance
full of honest water,
of the empty longing I see now is not my own,
but a common, durable sadness to be tempered by the waves,
forever rinsing and swallowing
all those accidental boulders.

From a California Housing Development

These acres composed of angular sunlight,
yellow grass, obdurate little flowers,
are in demand. Verandas, stucco walls,
foursquare chambers and dormers set
with soap-scribbled glass displace
the sky's brilliant volume. Though the valley's
circuitry has not yet climbed this foothill,
by September these rooms should fill
with laughter, conversations, nightgowns,
weeping, the reader's steady breathing.
Now the red roof tiles are stacked
like totems of exaggerated smiles.
Five months will finish the road, connect
the plumbing and power, turn the ruined
nails, papers, withered cactus under,
and work them into the succulent strips
watercolored on the scaled sketches.
Sprinklers will thresh the melting twilight.
From under this wide pastel sky, where
helicopters dig toward the moon; from
this arid hilltop's empty houses, I can only
send back abject vertigoes of longing.
Forgive me the times I have feigned sleep,
so as not to answer your whisper in the dark.

Uses of the Cedar

Sunlight leans across the path
between the rhododendrons.
Far down the gallery of cedars
the sea is breaking on the jetty.
I preserve the forest by remembering
the sound of the sea within it.

*

A white gate stopped with weeds
led from the orchard into woods.
A fungus called cedar apple
lived half its life on the shaggy
trunks, the rest on ripening apples.

*

Where was I?
You'd have found me in the cedar forest.

*

Cartier took saplings back to France.
Arbor vitae, it was proclaimed: a cedar
tea had cured his distempered crew.
The maps he made of the St. Lawrence
Valley are no longer true.

*

One afternoon we sawed up
boles of cedar until dusk.
The smell of a shirt left
for months in a drawer
retrieves the pink cores
of the logs, and intimates snow.
But is survival worth so little
in itself that it must be illustrated?
Whose life am I continuing?

*

The night the rain beat on the shingles,
Mittelberger listened. Out of cedar
he made the pipes of the new world's
first organ. No doubt someone has written
something for the instrument called rain.

*

One night with me you stepped out
of your clothes among the cedars.

*

The twisted one that stood in the field
beside the water is gone. Do you
understand when I say that wind
still seems to gather around its shape,
that this is not mere talk of ghosts?
We must believe the world can be remade.

*

Waxwing song is a needle, willing
the truth of you. Wait. They are about
to billow up from pliant cedartops,
vanish like a blade's edge, then veer
off all at once in a single wing.

*

A cedar sprig has remained
on my dresser seven months,
brittle but still green.
Because I cannot yet describe
its scored flat sprouts gracefully,
the cedar sprig refers me to the world.

★

From the white gate
look down to the jetty.

Nobody waits there.

★

Happiness is not made, but given.
It will never take that shape again.

The Carp That Swallowed a Diamond

In the hollow where April floods
have collected, tall thumb reeds
of grass stand on their reflections,
like sheaves bound at the still surface.
The sun is burning off its own dawn,
while the whine of eighteen-wheelers
hauling in tons of tropical fruit
or stiff new shoes downshifts into
the tangle of trees and rooftops.
Here in the park, beside this quiet
water meadow, the population's
habitual wakings, retrievals of life,
seem comfortably remote—until
the police car glides up and an officer
rolls down his window to say there's
been a housebreak one block west—
have I seen anything suspicious?
I shake my head. What's to suspect
in a flooded field? My heart's with
the thief anyway—maybe he's already
crossed the bridge and joined a crowd,
strolling with a purpose downtown;
maybe he's alone in some melancholy
kitchen drinking rye, having thrown
jewels from the bridge in a panic.
What is the use of hunting each
other's confessions down? The thief
makes off with the diamond because
a language evaluates its beauty,
gives it currency and weight;
there are words to imply all the layers
of light the diamond contains, and they
would translate into a holiday for life.
There is also a language of loss,

of everything unassuaged, that neither
the thief, nor his victim, nor I can
master yet. It would tell all, beginning
with the tale of the pumpkin-colored
carp, whose eyes are big as marbles,
and whose path across the hollow
is just now revealed, by trembling
stalks of grass in the fading mist.

Blueprint

Cornflowers have invested
the burned-out lot behind our house.
The realtor's fallen marquee
wastes a number on cirrus that speed
across the moon. The night we sat up
sweating out the blaze that made
this meadow is long gone by, but I can
still hear the sealed windows bursting,
the fire fighters shouting in that blind
back hall. Emerging later like divers
from a hulk, they said she and her dog
suffocated quickly in their sleep.
One pipe twists out of the weeds.
The driveway leads in and ends.
And fast clouds keep coming tonight,
a ceiling through which moonlight
quavers, turning all it touches abstract.
We've finished packing our belongings,
ready to move into morning. In our
old rooms a cool geometry measures
the vacant corners, but in this plot
of tall blue flowers, I find a poise,
a perfected tense, a place to be left behind.
Beyond those trees, in the house
where we have lived, a light burns
in my landlady's kitchen. The utility
drawer is open in there, a musty box
of string, tools, glue, useless bolts.
I was looking for a length of wire.
I was going to bind things up. But already
these vast clouds are bearing east,
smudging the hills with shadow.
Out over the North Atlantic, whole counties
of steam begin melting beneath the sun.

William Cowper

All evening I had been plodding through
the verse your century left behind,
after something symptomatic, something
in couplets, buffed, complacent, mythy
for display—to suggest Wordsworth was right,
that too often you all mistook the charming
surfaces of language for the heart that lay
refracted on the bottom, untouched. It was
arrogant, self-serving, but I wanted to make
a point, and it's easy being unfair to the dead.
You were different, of course, appealing
in your madness to us who see in madness
the authentic. You thought you were damned,
and so spent years beneath a preacher's spell,
a widow's companion, writing odes to furniture
at the whim of her haughty friends. Slight,
placid stuff, but occasionally moving. Plein-air
portions of "The Task" had tuned the aeolian harp.
That much I knew, but when I saw your "Epitaph
on a Hare," I thought I'd found the mock-heroic
meringue I had been hunting. Instead I learned
again the folly of whittling love's long labors
down to disputations of taste. Your poem gave
back April twilight after rain. On a Persian
carpet, the hare comes to suppressed pause
before the terrace doors. It seemed laughable
at first, reading this rabbit's requiem
two centuries later, noting his taste for pippins,
milk, and thistles. But then the parlor began
to furnish itself with dusk, darkening like
conscience, and when my eyes adjusted I could
see you there, motionless, consigned. Damned.
By shadows your sympathies resonate to, damned

because you know what's meant by *no health in us*.
You've less than the hare's eight brief years
left and you know it. I sat a long while, humbled
by the thought of your hands shredding bread,
as you were by the preacher's grim tenderness,
gravely turning the deckled pages of his book.

View from an Island, Dusk

Colors are the deeds and sufferings of light.
—Goethe

The bottle rocket went off twenty yards
Overhead, drifting down to them struck
Still there—shreds fell gently down
Beside his lover's child. And within him
A thousand discouragements converged.
The *bastards* up on the ridge slowly
Turned from their picnic plates to gape
At his little rage: shouts mixed up with
Gull cries. Nothing they couldn't smile off,
Some damn fool killjoy. Hadn't they
The high ground and plenty more rockets?

Then the child was clinging to her—
Both of them looked stunned, almost
Afraid. He didn't even understand himself.
But when he looks from the cottage porch,
Down the path they've beaten in the field,
The landscape has diminished and
Forgiven him. Blue stars define evening
Above the spruces, while he stares
At the cormorant on this morning's
Canvas, departing its dark reflection
On still water. What he had in mind,

What he was seeing just hours ago
Seems remote as childhood. He lugs his
Easel, brushes, knives, and rags inside,
Wondering over the colors he was mulling:
That umber, that violent green impasto.
Why was it he felt he owed so much
To the actual shapes of things? All these

Daydreamed landscapes, made of luminous
Distance and foregrounded idiosyncrasy:
The white hilts of leeks, the blue-green
Blades of their leaves, morning groundfog

Deer gingerly step through, the quiet
Invitations of her voice, music adrift
From yellow windows over midnight
Summer lawns. . . . "If you look after Kate,
I'll go get some lobsters. They've got
Fresh corn a ways up the road—have
We got wine?" She's asking from behind
The screen door beside him, avoiding
His eyes, he thinks. "Just a little red—
I'll put her down and help you cook
When you get back." "Can I," she says,

Stepping out at last, "take your bag?"
She lifts it from the hook and smiles.
After a minute shame, foreboding,
Silence get him up and around the corner
To watch her walk away. Hands in pockets,
Shoulders squared, she seems to him all
Thousand words she hasn't yet begun
To say about necessities and loss.
His eyes fill with dusk, watching her
Move off, recognizing beneath her clothes
The body he has loved, the odd lilt

Of her walk he will start at in a crowd.
He wonders if he hasn't too long
Mistaken mere attention for sympathy.
But who else could look at her so longingly,

And know she understands and begrudges
None of the comfort she's given him by
Becoming more mysterious, more known.
It will take a long time to release her
Secrets to the wind—the way she said
His name sadly or in laughter. *Can't you just*
Picture that, she'd say as they fell asleep.

He settles again in the rocker, beside
The fluttering trellis, his sunburned
Limbs suddenly chilled. And Kate comes
Quietly out in her nightgown to settle
In his lap, taking her thumb from her
Mouth to say, yes, I brushed my teeth.
He is happy she brings her need to trust
So readily in him—she knows him better
Than her own father. But that means
Nothing now. The long week here has been
Meant to tell him that. When up in the wind

The village steeple bells begin to blaze,
He can't explain—any more than he
Can say why his stomach has felt
So weak all day. Why, she asks him.
"I guess because today is special, the day
They signed the Declaration of Independence."
She's had it all explained to her before,
But he's remembering hearing once
That those who signed the document
Had not expected to, presumed there'd be
Some compromise. And those sycophant

Old masters of public oaths, of battlefields
Under burly clouds, even of those warm
Interiors, where the burgher family
Contents itself in firelight; they were paid
To promote the lie of grand ideals,
To keep us believing our lives belong
To purpose, will ripen into wisdom,
That kneeling on the shoulders of the dead
We're approaching heaven. Your mother
Doesn't love me anymore, he wants to say.
"Will they start the fireworks soon?"

"Not yet," he says, "but when they do,
If we can see them we'll get you up."
He can hear sleep overcoming her now,
Without tonight the same story, the same
Old book again, and though he is thankful,
He now can see why simple tales need
To be told repeatedly, why views of vales
And villages have to be painted: how else
Imagine certainty in a gathering darkness?
"When I was a boy," he says, "when father
Woke me in the morning, you know what

He'd say, he'd say— *Up, get up, the British
Are coming!* . . . Once he woke me up
At night, and you know where we went,
We went to a drive-in movie, me in my
Pajamas, snuck in free." "Really?" she asks,
Rousing a little, "in your pajamas,
In the trunk?" "No, silly, in the back seat,
Under a blanket." It occurs to him
That maybe there wasn't a charge for kids,

Maybe his parents were only trying
To make it seem more fun. . . . "So I fell

Asleep, so to sleep"—he's humming now,
Remembering the gentle curves and stops
The car made under him. She will never
Be his child. He will always be the friend
That families call *uncle*, onlooker in that
Arcadia he used to think anyone could
Make with freedom and work and love.
Family. Like those rocketeers this
Afternoon, whom they quietly observed
At last, so far away, packing up their
Celebration and straggling to their car.

He sees them now in caricature,
As pioneers, a family trudging west
Beside a wagon, lost among vast ocher
Plains and verges, immensities of sky,
Heading off, stampeding Oklahoma
For a claim. When they settle, hungers
Go on festering, the land gives out
And they move on, or maybe linger,
Rusting, warping. The last drive-in
He saw was in West Virginia slag hills,
Driving with his new wife home from

Honeymoon. It was back of their motel.
Out for a walk, they'd thought it would
Amuse to look on free. It was blue: a dozen
Cars huddled beneath a woman's crotch.
Her hips were twice the size of the ticket-
Taker's hut, and her loose breasts, her sallow

Face floated there in silence under stars.
That night they began to argue. Now
He cannot bring his ex-wife's face to mind,
Nor even hers, who will soon be home
With supper. Kate is fast asleep now,

And the wind has steadied, kindling
Streaks of orange above the mainland.
He lifts her gently, toes the screen door
Open and climbs the stairs. The channel
Buoy gleams in her window. Half-light,
Tenderness, her slow breathing on his
Shoulder give gradual shape to furniture
And toys. He smooths the blankets over her,
Held a moment by her doll's vacant eyes.
Three faces. Mother, child, doll. In the empty
House when they are gone, he will divide

Within, and join this bitter half in pointless
Talk, in long views from the follies
Of his life, out across the ocean's giant
Solitudes. He tucks the doll in beside her,
and tucks her hair behind the ear he
Whispers in—*good-bye*. Downstairs her
Mother rattles open a paper bag;
The corn squeaks out of its shucks. It's
More than he can face almost, the lobster
Steam, the wind, and now the distant
Soft report of fireworks over the mainland.

The restraint, the quiet talk by which
They'll arrive at their conclusion. Calm.
Why *did* he shout at those picnickers today?
Tomorrow at the ferry pier crowds of them

Will idle down from the saltbox hotels,
In billed caps and rumpled sportswear,
Some carrying the canvases they've bought,
As if anonymous staffage had traversed
A rendered distance, and stepped out
To pay for their vacation in a painting.
He will be going down to see them off

At last, to watch the ferry glide away
Beyond the cliff, into open ocean. He'll
Have another look at that iconic litter
Two fathoms down beneath the pier:
Aluminum window frames, a lawn rake,
A folding chair, a white enamel pot, all
Scattered over a backdrop of blue shingles.
Such things as he knows how to notice
Without her. At the doorway, once more
Watching thoughts pass across her face,
He thinks of his old idea to paint a series

Of common views: suds melting from a sink
Beside a dripping hand, a window shining
Through a wave of hair, idle feet and cool
Grass beneath a picnic table, framed
By the crook of an elbow. Why must love
Always end in promises made to himself,
To follow all over again the long divisions
Of light? She looks up at him at last, after
She's asked if Kate's asleep, after she's
Poured him the last of the warm red wine.

II

Rooms by the Sea

When I brought him back through the dark wing,
past ice-ferned windows to the hearth, he was
all questions about the harpoons and the portraits
on the walls. . . . We had come from the grim beach,

where edging out on the ice as far as we dared,
we saw this room's windows shining on the snow,
like the portholes of a ship trapped near the pole.
First sea ice in nearly thirty years. The house

has become a kind of diary: maps yellow on the wall,
the Great War's cruisers still penciled at their berths.
The barometer holds steady season after season.
Just last month, mother gave me one of her hideous

brooches, a pair of her squat shoes. She's come
to think of me now as a spinster sister—she hopes
the church will engage me. I'm not sure she doesn't
suspect he is a ghost. Even I have wondered if the man

who's fallen asleep beside me here was really the cat
that came affectionately, darkly, instead of him
to a rendezvous one night. I am a creature of half-beliefs,
a fool for superstitions. Watching him sleep, I could

believe in whatever I can make of him: *He's come*
to see that I survive somewhere far from here.
He's come to fall asleep beside this fire. With every
meal mother eats more slowly, and lately never tires

of her winter's tale—1901, her first year with father.
Iceboats like spiders on white linen, fabulous fish
hauled up from holes . . . various dogs and the minister's
child drifted seaward on one big block, and your father

saved them, in that skiff (now turtled on stumps,
shelter for grackles rummaging sunflower seeds).
Because the light is best from the east, she holds
that old head still some mornings, shuts her eyes,

and has me pull new hairs from her chin — the only
vanity I've ever known in her. Afterwards I walk
a long way down the beach, and my hands keep finding
their way to my face. She laughed at me last month,

when I wouldn't say whom I was baking for. "Dumb-cake,"
she said. "You're baking dumb-cake. If you keep quiet,
not a word 'til it's done, the story goes, he'll marry you!"
(A peasant ritual she'd read of — she meant comfort,

but I had no magical intentions.) One night just
after father went, she dragged me out in my nightgown
in December, to see the aurora pleating the sky.
She had to drag me in again. The fine gold hairs

on my thighs stood up while I rubbed away the cold.
That night in the lamplight I looked beautiful to myself.
Where was your hope, mother? Is that what you tucked
into father's hand as he lay in the satin box? What

matter anyway? Haven't I given painless injections,
worked for the vote, taught little ones to read?
Where there is life . . . She's past the point of wishing me
gone, well-married — she thinks she needs me here,

But I must go. The fire's down, and he sleeps soundly
now, maybe dreaming of the ice we crept across,
disbelieving in five solid inches of salt water. That
black buoy, solemnly tilted in the harbor's pale field,

would be my coat of arms if not for him. Out there,
I was falling back into myself, so far that I could see us
as one sees back over decades . . . will he remember
the star we saw sprint from the sky? All these years

the moon's been turning in my blood, empty, patient.
Never have I yearned like this before. Sometimes
in my sleep I become a clumsy diver, and when doors
I'm pawing open, faces I have known slowly turn,

revealing walleyes, the tusks of a boar. Or my own
obtuse figure faces me, slipstreaming chains.
How I have longed to feel well enough to be bored,
to know real fear (that thick black insect on the spine).

I remember watching father let the dogs in from a storm.
Naked, fish-white in the shadows, he opened the door,
and rain gleamed beside the jamb. The dogs burst in
on mother's homely sleep, on gritty paws, black mouths

slit back to the molars, panting, shaking. . . . Now his
dreaming hand squeezes mine—how strange to think
my lover's hand. Soon a mere pulse will survive of us.
We'll lie here 'til morning, never more a man and woman

together than tonight, at the foot of this old chimney,
one pipe for the wind, blowing west in the faces of angels.

The Age of Discovery

When I look down along the blanket's soft
Swell over you, as if downhill toward
A hidden harbor, I wonder if on the sunlit
Side of the earth you might be wading,
In a gentle turquoise surf, your dress

Caught up in hand. Wet fronds hung like green
Machetes from the ceiling, when our friend
Lit up his slides of Guadalcanal on our wall.
After the black volcanic sand, the warplane
Wreckage, the betel juice and red-feather money,

People of the last carousel stared in at us.
Rain strafed the puddles they stood in ankle-deep,
Glazing black the hair of children who had just
Received their ceremonial nose rings. So much
Of the world threatens to remain imaginary

That the downpour on the window all night
Sufficed to join us, at least in knowing there is
A blind *within* to everything, and no place
That doesn't make its own sound, meeting rain.
Why do I want to tell you now how strange

The skating pond was in summer, when green
Lampshades still hung from wires over
The wrinkling water? What spins out the endless
Skein of harlequin scarves I go on hauling up
With hopeless pleasure on indolent afternoons

Or sleepless nights? In the dark, breathing
Room questions rise all the way to my lips,
But I do not wake you, within whom someone else
Is taking shape, even now. Someone who will
Outlive us, witnessing the end of expeditions

We supposed were dreams. And it is pleasing
Now to summon up a beach's empty canvas,
Whitecaps smoking along the bar, and that tiny
Brig I had as a boy, under crisp yellow sail,
Its course steadfastly set out of the bottle.

Landscape for an Antique Clock

This morning I read the cottage diary, hoping to find
Peculiar things from that world we've seen in photographs,
Or even partially recall: pumped water's frigid chuckle

Into a soapstone sink, wing-walkers, steam locomotives,
Deliveries of milk bottles with shirred paper caps.
But she was only moved to write of meals, and parades

For doughboys restored to their lives, her expectations
Of strawberries, clarities of weather— *Today the haze
Burned off by ten and we could see Mt. Washington*—

Nothing I could read the historical future into, nothing
It seemed worth reimagining. Why should I care that her days
Here were merely tonic, curative perhaps, of another life

She never saw fit to mention; that she failed to remark
The artifacts and symptoms of her era; that only
Fresh suppers and company brought her joy? The diary

Came with the place when the current owner bought it,
A curiosity, or as perhaps the realtor suggested, a quaint
Authentication. The sunlight this morning is a plain truth

Complicated, like an aphorism revolved in its retellings.
Under flouncing birches, an overalled farmer glides
Above the hedge between a pair of huge red tractor wheels.

He turns in his seat and waves so earnestly. When I wave
Back the porch swing trembles and a few of her pages turn
Haphazardly in the air. Make yourself at home, the owner

Said when he left; make yourself a home, I thought, make
Yourself home. Now that I have read her artless history,
I'll sit here well past noon, wondering how long the wind

Will have to blow to strip the hedge of those white petals.
I will watch that lobster boat patiently circle the cove,
And the periodic glint of sun on its practical cabin windows.

At a Sunday Concert

After the young man's seizure, the afternoon
took on a different tone. His friends just
managed to drag him from the chamber;
as his oxfords disappeared behind a column,
your fingertips completed the puzzled glance
we shared, feathering the skin of my inner wrist.
To stare would have been rude, so we turned
back to the soloist, who menaced the piano
during orchestral interludes. But gradually
the room began to seem the fragile system
of dependencies it was: posts and lintels, balconies,
chandeliers, handed down just so from invisible
joists and iron bolts no thicker than a finger.
Even the strings, so carefully troubled into melody,
relied on principles to make their harmonies.
Scores the players leaned toward were measuring
how long, how long until the cello insinuates
its mournful theme, how long before they'd all
agree to finish and the room begin to empty.
The music was made to dissolve—it came to pass
on the air, just as did the vague light that said not
long, not long before some rain, before the friends
would ease him into bed, remove the handkerchief
from his mouth, compose his hands and ask if
there was anything he needed. We were already
walking beneath an umbrella to the car. A man
folding chairs was stooping after somebody's
white glove. And then, like one who takes his eye
from a gunsight, relinquishing the cross hairs
for a flurry of windy leaves, for the whole
chaotic horizon, I was lost, love, given back
to my brief and fortunate life, to chance,
whose laws gave me to you so long ago, and hold.

History
for Arden

Every spring, Gordon, my father's old
Shipmate, would find us grade-school boys
A ship to roam. One year we actually sailed
To Providence from Boston on a destroyer.
But by noon our interest in gadgets gave
Way to hide-and-seek; the ship became
Another place where we were boys. I suppose
We steered some, manned the guns, or stood
In the engine room's quivering, oiled air
With patient sailors. But I best recall
Sitting astern, watching our wake pacify
The water beneath swarms of hungry gulls.

Twenty years later that view still seems
A strange reconnaissance, my only way
To imagine father's long look back to San Diego,
1950, or the yearning of great-uncle Claudius
Toward France and the shell that would kill him
Four weeks shy of Armistice. Why wish this back?
I want my conscience comprehensive, open
To the past; and sometimes savoring regrets
Or resolutions, or flushed and pleasantly
Aching after some sunny game, I think myself
Fortunate, even blessed. I want to imagine
Those who gave me life as generous, and their

Lives as more than blocks of stone from
Which only agonized parts emerge distinctly,
Like Michelangelo's slaves from their marble.
What were our fathers thinking of—to take us
Aboard that ship? Were they nurturing our
Martial fascinations, or just redeeming
The site of their worst terrors, through a Sunday
Outing with the boys? Who was responsible

43

For us—whose head would have rolled had
One of us drowned? I know no more than they did,
When as youths they snapped their palms up
Smartly to their brows and the ship swung away

From the pier toward death. I can't ignore them,
Though I have tried, though I recognize their
Naïveté and my own, in its cool disguise.
They haunt me, like the neighbor's son
Who went down on *Thresher*. Photographs
Of wreckage, like broken tubes of ash
From a neglected cigarette, gave me nightmares
For a month. Over and over, fathoms down,
The sallow lantern of father's face would hang
Out of reach. I never told him this—supposing
That willingness to die for an idea was beyond me,
That my questions would embarrass bravery.

What was my father thinking of? Survival?
Or freedom, as some philosopher defined it—
In recognition of necessity? This century
Has made the earth an automated abattoir,
Which memory serves alike to justify, refuel.
Now that I have spent years examining ideas,
Suspecting ignorance or misprision in every
Call to arms, I look back, as off the stern
Of that destroyer, as if I could understand.
I will never really know what my father
Was thinking of, although I could pretend to.
When they drew my high number from the bowl,

It was over, and as symptomatic of my time
As father was of his, I'd already convinced myself
Imagination is the truest form of conscience.
But my beliefs cost me nothing. Evidence
Accumulates and melts like snow, like shredded
Government documents that filled a city side
Street for a festival last summer, two feet deep,
Delighting children. What are my beliefs but
Aesthetical suspicions—that the beautiful,
The virtuous, the true are just the vital
Obverse of the filth that tyrants and death
Return us to. . . . The beautiful *are* losers.

All is eventually lost. Heroes swim
The current to keep us mindful of that loss.
But these are not convictions—more like
Sentimental susceptibilities to music
Or to pine trees raked with wind; like a fierce
Belief in spirits that yields an attic full
Of clothes and broken chairs. At thirty,
Spared, I'm reckoning my position without
Charts, with only anecdotes that loom in me
Like legends, based on pure contingency.
Twenty years after the shell took Claudius,
His sister watched a hurricane flood

Providence with her son, my father.
As the water subsided, a wailing grew
In the wind, pitched above it half a tone
Gathering voice from all the ravaged streets:
Dozens of shorted auto horns were blowing.
Now they linger like a faint inflammation
Of the skull, warning me of disasters
Already suffered and overgrown. I look out

45

Across the town, into the underwater light
That comes before a storm, and remember
Gordon drowned off Falmouth ten years ago.
Father stays up late in my old room,

Reading Hakluyt's *Voyages*. Perhaps
His sleep is troubled still with the cries
Of men who struggle in a sea made of fire.
That old destroyer, long since scrapped,
Has been reforged—swifter and more lethal.
Somewhere overhead, the Command Post plane
Called *Looking Glass* circles like a blind,
Phlegmatic shark. What were our fathers
Thinking of? Wind from a long ways off
Begins whirling in the trees. Between
Preliminary fits of rain and lightning,
The rooftops afterimage as ruined stairs.

Museum

It's fiercely sunny in the room you've found
Yourself within. Someone they wished to seem
Frugal and modest must have slept off renown

In the canopy bed. The floor has slanted
Into a settlement the foundation has at last
Arranged with the meadow, and stranded

In the window's rippled glass, an apple's old
Knuckles bristle with second growth. Over
The lavender ridge two silent clouds unfold.

It is your face in the tarnished mirror,
Your hand closing on the bone-handled comb.
But apparently no one can see you here—

No one ever will—in this tiny antique room,
Roped off with plush red velvet. On the bed's
Soft, inviting edge you gratefully sit down,

And slowly unlace your old shoes, gazing
Down upon them the way a parachutist sees
Desert mountains pass beneath his knees.

Having All Night

The darkness I believe in falls at last,
Soothing and explaining my confusions as mere
Weather paling leaves, as salutary rituals
Like boiling snow for tea, erotic transformations

To culminate on the tongue, and in such fragrance.
Having read the book on your dresser right up
To your bookmark, groping as into a glove,
I am sure we will survive, and that my wandering

Will first disclose a man in a window, carefully
Rolling his sleeves before a piano, a tin can
Rattling down a brook, breeze filling the leaves,
And across the harbor all the lights burning.

Night is the kingdom we discover after childhood's
Centuries of sleep. I shall walk it out again,
Like a prince disguised, making observations
Of his realm. How happy I shall be tonight, happy—

Though I will hear a woman weeping in her yard,
And curses flung from a car; though I disappointed
You today, there is redemption in this residential
Evening, and the surf of this wind will break as stars.

On Leaving a Demonstration to Have My Hair Cut

after Thoreau

We were all wearing black,
    and so the sun beat into us
whatever we believed—heat
    turned us resolute as the patriot
we were gathering beneath.
    A young megaphonist asked
who'd carry bodies—pillows
    buttoned into clothes—
in memory of civilians our funding
    of insurgency had killed.
This was penance and objection—
    that's how most of us would have
put it, but some placards
    embarrassed me: our congressman was
not a murderer, just something
    of a dupe. The government was
acting like a government again.
    We were just withholding our
complicity again. So we slowly
    marched the morning out before
our fellow citizens, who watched us
    with that studied, condescending air
the museumgoer has before
    period-costumed mannequins
of forebears dipping candles,
    reading prayers. It was like
traveling into a farther
    country, so tolerant, so certain
of its enveloping good fortune,
    that its bankers shed their jackets
in the sun, and in their blinding
    shirtsleeves bore us witness.
At a plaza, beneath another
    vigilant bronze, we settled in for

speeches. My appointment
      loomed. The sun glared down
on my shaggy neck. If I kept her
      waiting, she would miss her lunch,
and I make it a point not to annoy
      anyone wielding scissors.
So I took off my black coat,
      and idly combing fingers across
my scalp, edged away—into
      mere enjoyment of an opinion,
into the crowd, beginning,
      yes, to comprehend just what its
inhabitants were about.

A Postcard in Memory of Donald Evans

Walking past a boatyard full of cradled sloops
last night, I thought of you. Yellow portholes
yielded the shoulders of someone doing delicate
work, floating perhaps, above a coast he hopes
he will explore, or stilting his compass across
the pale deeps. Three just-varnished blocks
beaded a rope across the cockpit. In the flat
surrounding fields, luminous local vegetables
hide beneath dark leaves, and on the pier
at evening, piles of red-needled sea urchins,
swung from a trawler's hold, pour loudly
into a truck. But the stolid, mumbling, upwind
flight of the blimp each morning most brings
you to mind—outward bound for Nadorp,
Iles des Sourds, Mangiare. Most of your countries
had just achieved independence, or had steadily
reclaimed themselves from cold ocean and sky.
They linger at the margins of our maps.
Canceled on yellowed envelopes, or fixed
like stars to black collector sheets, tinctured
in the watercolor you said could not be labored,
their stamps commemorate our love of minor
beauties, perishable things. In the full panes
of your exotic issues, made of tiny, certain strokes
and pastel fogs, I recognize myself, the boy
who wanted everything arrayed, passed through
imagination's tender lens, orderly as the leaded
green and mustard meadows tilting on a wingtip,
where long archipelagoes of shadow slowly drift.

Your Left Hand
for Rory

I'd listen through the wall between our rooms,
above the kitchen where a pitcher of tea
crimsoned all day in the window. The flora had half
a season left to descant on their comprehensive
unisons of green. You wouldn't be disturbed:
the same blue notes, the same half-dozen
choruses strummed out beneath your voice—
urgent, then retiring, then climbing all over again
the ladder of chords. Nobody would ever ask you
what time it was, but you knew it needed shaping.
While I painted model airplanes, read sullen books
or mooned, you were already at it: conjugating,
declining, shaping time to a course, as we'd shape
wind those days in sails, spilling it a moment
luffing up, then recollecting it suddenly as
a new tack heeled in. Sinister, sinistra, sinistrum.
Now your left hand knows its way along
those four thick strings, into the tune's pivotal
shadows—moving, sliding on back up to walk
on down again, and when your right hand is
demonstrating the virtual beauty of silence,
the rhythm's opened wing, the left's already found
the note to come, pausing near its curved edge,
waiting. Time, time. At seven we hated
each other, cousin, then found our way together
in the dark, walking miles in our pajamas.
A ship that filled the channel we'd first hear
in our feet—and risk an open moonlit field
to watch its huge black hull pass by.
Summer nights were worth the mornings
we exchanged for sleep. As my right hand
moves across this page, you are driving
a third set through some nightclub's thick,

electrical air. Our long morning is already over—
thirty years. We couldn't have just dreamed
our way to this meridian. Pick up that big,
voluptuous fiddle—measure us out some more.

Contrition

The stranger I passed at high
Speed on the early autumn
Highway: who can say what
Song she was singing so loudly

In her old sedan? As the needle
Edged into the record, I heard
Shuffling on the bandstand,
And from stageside somebody's

Voice: *So I will see you again*
Tomorrow? The tenorman's
Breath dissolved the answer,
Like a pattern that won't return

To a kaleidoscope for years.
And from a train's rear window
I have seen bridge after bridge
Flung down in a blaze of sunset.

I do not love her now, nor
Would I. We are each other's
Camphored secrets, nearly
Forgotten. We fend for ourselves.

But what spirits have been
Using me, while rain was
Inspiring all these old green
Leaves. I dozed, and there

She was, standing under
Clouds, surrounded by those
I'd since made promises to.
What makes me grieve failing

Her so long ago—what kept me
From taking her tired face
In my hands and thumbing away
The eyelash from her cheek . . .

Night Game

Nobody's just watching, not those perched
on a billboard beyond the center-field fence,
not the paid attendance, not the manager
thinking through his roster in the dugout,
slowly clapping. In a verdant block of light
carved out of evening, the game patiently
proceeds to discover its own dimensions.
Across the diamond, beyond the upper deck,
huge glass towers sheer into darkness.

Joy will make waves in thousands of people.
Lesser occasions—sudden fouls, foreign
scores, chin music—register on the crowd's
broad face like smiles donated to keep up
conversation. Two pale clouds have anchored
near the flag, whose broad stripes swell
and then subside. In the press box shirtsleeved
men look on like admirals from a bridge,
translating each habitual scuffing of spikes
or cap adjustment into megahertz of tension.

The pitcher stalks behind the mound, kneading
the ball, wiping his brow with a forearm.
A gentle wish of blue smoke hangs over his head.
At last he leans in, like one admonishing a child
who has stumbled into trouble he might have
avoided. Precision richly mixed with accident
has left two on, two out, two—nothing for
the home team in the ninth. Gull shadows flicker
over the poised infield. As he begins his toppling
stride, the pitcher reaches into his glove,

plucking as out of a hat the ball and slings it
suddenly home. And it is emphatically
reversed, rising into the lights, into darkness.
In the bat's risen arc of follow-through
there's an instant nobody solves, not the hitter
already shedding his weapon and starting
to run, not the pitcher strangely dancing down
to back up the plate. The center fielder trots back

and turns, spreading his capable arms open in greeting.

The Pose
for Georgia

Remember the sculptor you modeled for—
the long afternoons at his estate?
All his precious metals deny my tenses now,
the drift of recollection this depends on,
but I would like to tell you anyway,

give back that day to you as it has come
to linger in me. I could begin with proverbs,
or with peacocks: something about poverty
and love and jealousy, the armatures I took
for inspiration. I'd have clothed us all so

truthfully in words. But now I think
that bird, opening the hundred eyes
of its plumage, and the squalls it gave out
all afternoon furnish a better entrance.
Unable to make any literate use

of the pastoral time he'd provided,
I dozed in a hammock, or toured the grounds,
discovering his pieces: a bronze deer
curled up on a brambled hillside,
a four-foot iron locust poised beside a hedge.

He'd rifled creation, as if before the scales
of things had been assigned, and set these
beasts in his cool woods for pleasure.
I began to wonder what he would make
of your earnest face, the difficult moods

of your eyes, the grace you had, undressed.
Of course he would avoid those eyes.
Hadn't I? I had not even learned to say

what happened as it had, and so I envied
his dominion over surfaces and shadows.

When later he asked me into the studio,
I stared at the sketches and Polaroids
he'd taken of his people, animals, insects—
where did the spirit live in all that flesh?
Huge moths, their wings mooned with azure,

hung in velvet-lined cases on the wall.
Bare-chested like a deckhand, his apprentice
was buffing a peacock of hammered bronze
and copper, its tail furled in a long heavy arc.
Wiping his hands on a smock, the artist smiled,

and said, "Why don't you walk around it.
I'm letting it take its own course now—
as a writer you know what I mean."
You had been swimming back into the arms
of your shirt; now I felt your hand

in mine and was grateful. We edged around
the image: too heavy-hipped, I thought.
One arm was crossed behind its back,
the left akimbo, caught in a kind of swagger.
One foot bore five articulated toes; the other

had yet to emerge from plastic wrapping.
Some wasted clay was stuck on the flank.
He had found the fine severity of your gaze,
but the wide, unfocused eyes and parted lips
strained after sound, as if muted in a dream

the figure's pose did not belong in.
Everything I feared in you was in that stance,
that body declaring itself alone, but love
did seem a way to soothe its empty cry.
I must have said something, but today,

having found the program for the show
in which the cast head alone sold for thousands,
I don't know what it was. He carefully fit
a bag over the figure. He had to think it over.
For a while. Next Saturday perhaps?

Rain had begun to mutter in the leaves,
and the peacock had strutted for shelter.
Pity took hold of me, for the deer
in the woods—for his presumption and my
own, our attempts to draw the spirit

up to the skin and hold it there,
in pewter, in a blush of poetry or memoir.
This afternoon, looking at your rumpled
dress flung over a chair, I recall
that he meant to clothe the figure,

but it never seemed to work. He moved on
to something different. We moved away.
Eight years later, sunlight burnishes our bed.
And I am still happily abashed to be waiting
on the love your empty dress is promising.

Toward Hallowe'en

I woke in painted stillness and stepped
out on the porch. The silted altitudes were
motionless, and although it hadn't rained,
the light was melancholy, damp, made
for still black boughs and brilliant leaves.
One of those days that deserves its very
own name: Latin for air-without-motive,
autumn-holding-steady. I stared into
the trees, as a child looks into a picture
said to contain a tiger's smile, a five-
pointed star, a domino, a hand—when with
a sound like distant applause (fainter
than the softball crowds who had rejoiced
all summer beyond the trees), one whole
maple's wild red leaves poured down
across the street. No wind, no bird, no
squirrel, just a steady shower of leaves
from a stolid tree, so sudden and unanimous
it seemed deliberate. Standing there,
my arms embossed with bedding wrinkles,
I was pierced with recognition acute
and inexplicable as the sweet, focused
ache a finger held inches from my forehead
provokes. I didn't know why—but that
was *joy*—release from having to stitch
effect to cause, from having to name each
five-fingered leaf or separate day. They
would fall away in good time, from places
in a picture of the past, into a hushed,
mysterious storm of bright red leaves.

Upon a Fit of Laughter

The minor guffaw the columnist
Hoped to elicit pops open
Like a jug and begins to pour.

It's not that funny. But oh,
The quiet house starts filling
All the same, the windows

Wide open on the morning's
Enlightenment. Surely
As water climbs a hose to seek

A deeper stillness, it mumbles
And puffs up out of me,
And its foolish song drifts

Over the neighborhood.
The more I will it silent,
The louder it becomes, finally

Diminishing to that dry,
Staccato cough so prized by
Comics. What's gotten into

You, my mother used to ask.
I have to wonder. I still
Believe divinity lives in

Laughter, not the cruel
Burst and bellow of a crowd,
But the inexplicable, up-

Welling dance in one body,
Or the bacchic two-step with
Someone who was there.

As children, we'd lie down
After tag at dusk, our heads
On each other's bellies,

Waiting for tremors to walk
Through us all and back,
And that first small laugh was

Deliverance, passed among us,
Gathering us, on that cool
Green lawn beneath the stars.

Seventh Month

When the wind swung east among the treetops,
and shadows began to layer the woods, we knew
we'd be lighting the lamps inside an hour.
Our waiting had just distilled as apprehension,
trouble our talk had finally shaped from months
of wary silence. Like a threatened dreamer,
I had imagined my way up safe among the rafters,
where already it was dusk and easy to imagine
unanswerable sorrow. Old deities reassembled
in my head, perched as fish crows in the dead
gray trees along the beach. Oh, I would atone
for every scrap of luck life had tossed me.
Alone in the woods at seven months we had
at last acknowledged an ancient tribulation
that love might help assuage. But it was still
a self-regarding fiction, trivial beside
the suffering a child could endure in a world
demanding straight limbs, twenty digits,
eyes and ears alert. All morning I'd been
matching leaves to a field guide, admiring
a wild iris, and a platter of orange fungus
fastened to a spruce trunk. Even then, this
faintly obscene remorse for the possible
was taking hold of me, becoming a pure self-
pity nature seemed disinclined to speak to.
We had made up lists of names in the sunlight—
inconclusive spells. What we'd have to show
for love was already more like the secretive
hungers we heard in the forest at night.
Now the moon was focusing over the trees,
having hauled the cold tide into earshot.
At last you stood heavily up and led me down
to watch the weir vanish, the foul ledges
dissolve into rumors. Strong water: our feet

blanched in it, ached, and then forgot themselves.
Under its whirl the muscular stones were clean
and beautiful. So we sat through dusk together,
watching the white conclusions of the waves.

About the Author

Robert Farnsworth is a visiting assistant professor of English at Colby
College. He has taught at Ithaca College, SUNY Cortland, and SUNY
Binghamton and was an instructor for the New York State Poets in the
Schools Program and for the Art Without Walls program at the Arthur
Kill Correctional Facility on Staten Island. Farnsworth's first book,
Three or Four Hills and a Cloud, was published by Wesleyan in 1982. A
graduate of Brown University (B.A. 1976) and Columbia University
(M.F.A. 1979), Farnsworth has also served as assistant poetry editor of
Antaeus and worked as a bookseller in Ithaca. He was awarded an NEA
grant for 1989–1990. His home is in Lewiston, Maine.

About the Book

Honest Water was composed in Bembo, a typeface adapted from the
Monotype version of an Aldine Roman cut before 1500 by Francesco
Griffo, who later designed the first italic type. It is named for Griffo's
contemporary, the humanist scholar Pietro Bembo. The book was
composed by Marathon Typography Service, Inc. of Durham, North
Carolina. It was designed and produced by Kachergis Book Design of
Pittsboro, North Carolina.